GOURD LIGHTS

How to Make 9 Beautiful Lamp and Lantern Projects

SUSAN NONN

4880 Lower Valley Road • Atglen, PA 19310

Other Schiffer Books by the Author:
Cut-out Gourd Techniques, ISBN 978-0-7643-4296-7

Other Schiffer Books on Related Subjects:
Creating Wall Pockets: 10 Gourd Projects to Paint and Hang, Sammie Crawford,
ISBN 978-0-7643-5020-7

Wax on Gourds: Decorative Techniques for Transforming Gourds & Rims, Miriam Joy,
ISBN 978-0-7643-5225-6

Creative Embellishments for Gourd Art, Marianne Barnes,
ISBN 978-0-7643-4492-3

Designed by RoS
Cover design by RoS
Type set in Stymie/Chaparral Pro

ISBN: 978-0-7643-5429-8
Printed in China

Published by Schiffer Publishing, Ltd.
4880 Lower Valley Road
Atglen, PA 19310
Phone: (610) 593-1777; Fax: (610) 593-2002
E-mail: Info@schifferbooks.com
Web: www.schifferbooks.com

For our complete selection of fine books on this and related subjects, please visit our website at www.schifferbooks.com. You may also write for a free catalog.

Schiffer Publishing's titles are available at special discounts for bulk purchases for sales promotions or premiums. Special editions, including personalized covers, corporate imprints, and excerpts, can be created in large quantities for special needs. For more information, contact the publisher.

We are always looking for people to write books on new and related subjects. If you have an idea for a book, please contact us at proposals@schifferbooks.com.

Contents

To my family and friends, who support, encourage, and tease me

about my obsession with gourds.

Acknowledgments

While the author of this book is identified as Susan Nonn, it is the result of collaboration with numerous individuals.

Thank you, Marilynn Draxl, for correcting my words, believing in me, and being a photographer for a day. Thanks to my sister, Ada Jayne, who gave up her days off to photograph the projects at Schiffer Publishing. Terry Noxel also was a photographer for a day, and was kind enough to bring a car filled with lamps to photograph for the book's gallery of artists. Jayne Wright not only was a photographer for a day, but also taught me how to decoupage.

I want to thank my brothers, Tony and Michael, for their knowledge and patience as I learned how to construct lamps. Both provided their expertise and time in helping me master the assembly of my lamps.

Most of all, I thank all of the gourd artists who generously contributed to the inspirational gallery.

My first "gourd gift." My mother bought it at the Florida Gourd Society's Festival in 1998.
Unfortunately there is no signature on the gourd to recognize the artist.

Introduction

Writing about gourd lamps introduced me to the world of simple electrical wiring. I spent afternoons at my public library reading back issues of *Handyman* instead of losing myself in fiction. There are few books written about basic lamp construction, but I do recommend *The How-To Book of Repairing, Rewiring, and Restoring Lamps and Lighting Fixtures* by Rachel Martens. Although written in 1979, it includes a glossary that allowed me to do online research for lamp parts. My glossary is based on my interpretation of Marten's, and I included some images to help clarify certain terms.

Another good way to learn is by attending seminars at building supply stores. Lowes and Home Depot offer seminars on electrical wiring. Although these focus on household wiring, the speakers were kind enough to answer my questions, so don't be shy about asking your own questions.

Also, look to people you know for advice. My best source for "hands-on" knowledge was my brothers. They were incredibly patient when I showed up with my box of lamp pieces.

There are so many construction questions that have to be considered when creating a lamp.

- Are you using a gourd as a base?
    - *How will it stand?*
    - *How will you weight it so it doesn't topple over?*
    - *How will you run/hide the wiring?*
    - *How will you fasten the socket?*
- Are you using a gourd as a shade?
    - *How will it be attached?*
    - *How will it balance?*
- What is the proportion between the base and the shade?
- Is it safe?
- How will your lamp turn on and off?

Safety and the Law

In the United States, Underwriters Laboratories, Inc. inspects electrical products. Lamps, lighting fixtures, lampshades, and lamp parts that have been certified safe bear the UL stamp of approval. Obtaining UL approval for handmade lamps can cost thousands of dollars and involve annual fees.

An alternative to creating handmade lamps is to assemble a lamp using UL-approved electrical units. In the Resources section, you will find complete units (plug, wire, switch, and socket) listed that you can assemble to make glow lights, pendants and swags, sconces, and table lights.

A second alternative is to buy lamp fixtures with shades or globes that can easily be replaced with your own gourd creations. Even in this instance, while the lamp itself will be UL approved, the shade will not, which can cause problems if your intent is to sell your work. If you sell an unapproved lamp part, you remain liable, although people do it all the time.

I have included a project to make a lamp using all UL-approved pieces except for the gourd lampshade. If I intend to sell a lamp such as this, I appeal to my neighbor, a master electrician, to do the simple wiring for me.

It is important to be responsible and to understand that there are legal issues regarding selling electrical products.

Basic Tools for Electric Work

When I started working on gourd lights, I thought I would need to invest in another array of tools. Fortunately, I had few additional tools to buy.

A good hacksaw is important. The most common problem with building a lamp is cutting the threaded lamp pipe for a smooth, even edge. A simple way to avoid a metal burr is to screw a locknut on each side of the cut. After the lamp pipe is cut, just twist the locknuts out. This process will remove any metal burr at the edge of the cut pipe.

I thought I needed an extra long (and very expensive) ⅜" drill bit but it wasn't necessary. A normal ⅜" drill bit worked on every one of my projects.

You will need a Phillips head and a standard (flat-head) screw driver, and a circular cutter. The circular cutter does not cut the threaded pipe, but works well on copper tubing.

Other tools you'll need for the projects are basic gourd tools: a mini jig-saw, sanders, drill, and a Dremel® rotary tool.

Gourd Preparation

There are two basic steps to prepare a raw gourd for any project:

- *Remove dirt and mold from the outer shell.*

- *If opening the gourd, clean and smooth the inside surface.*

Try to buy gourds that have been cleaned of the majority of dirt and mold. Sometimes you'll start with a gourd that isn't very clean. Most dirt and mold can easily be removed with dish detergent, a small amount of bleach and a copper scrubby. Check your gourd to make sure your scrubby does not leave scratches. If there is a lot of mold, soak the gourd and scrape the surface with a peeling knife.

Some gourds have a hard white mold that is very difficult to remove. If the gourd has this type of mold cover it in non-chemical potting soil for a few days. The potting soil loosens the mold and I am able to clean the gourd with my peeling knife and copper scrubby.

If the inside of a gourd needs to be cleaned, be careful not to inhale the contents. The insides will contain dust and possible mold/fungus. People working with gourds talk about contracting "gourd flu" with symptoms such as feverish aching joints, muscle soreness, mucus, and fatigue that lasts for a few days.

If I am cleaning a lot of gourds at one time, I fill them with water and wait two to three days. The inside membrane is then easily removed by scraping with a large canning lid. If that doesn't work, I repeat the process. My last step is to refill the gourd first with a bleach solution and then vinegar to turn the interior shell to a consistent white. It does take a few days of good weather to dry the gourd again. After the gourd is dried I use a sanding star on the interior to achieve a smooth surface.

Sometimes I don't have time to clean interiors with water. If a few gourds need cleaning I use a concrete ball or carbide cleaner with my drill. Both these tools will rough up the interior, so the last step is to use a sanding star.

Safety: Remember both the outer shell and interior membrane of a gourd have mold and dust. Cleaning loosens these and they become airborne. It is important to wear dust masks and work in a well-ventilated area.

Planning Your Design

Once your gourd is clean, it's time to design. Gourds can be nightlights, pendants, swags, wall sconces, table lamps or floor lamps. Before you start to construct a light/lamp, you need to make some basic decisions, especially before you cut out the gourd's top, bottom, or side. Knowing what type of light/lamp you want to make is very important.

After deciding on which lighting fixture to create, you need to consider design elements. Color is the first thing I think of when visualizing a finished light. I can paint, dye, ink, or burn a gourd to add color. I can ap-preciate the natural color of a gourd and wax to highlight its surface patterns. If you are creating a gourd light/lamp for your home, it's easy to match color to the room's décor.

Surface design is another decision: a gourd can be drilled, carved, and/or cut. You can add embellishments to your gourd light/lamp for texture. Examples of embellishments could be netless knotting, molding with clay, beading, or a basketry technique.

Below are some processes I have tried on a gourd light that I would like to share with you.

Designing with Holes

Gourd lamps can be made with a drill and different size drill bits. The light shining through the holes creates incredible patterns on surrounding surfaces. On thick gourds the smaller holes will not reflect as well and the angle of the hole also affects light. I draw/drill circular designs using Miriam Joy's rubber templates.

If I want a more complex/realistic pattern I would use a computer application that manipulates vector based images. For example, I used Adobe Fireworks to change this blue butterfly into a dotted image.

To Bead or Not to Bead

A popular technique is to plug some or all the holes with round glass or acrylic/plastic beads. I prefer acrylic beads because they are so light. Most beads are measured with the metric system. Using a millimeters-to-inches table I found on the internet (http://www.metric-conversions.org/length/millimeters-to-inches.html) helps me match my drill bits to bead size.

To avoid using glue, the bead has to fit snuggly in the hole. Most of the time, I was able to press the bead firmly into the hole with my thumb. To avoid getting a sore thumb, use the eraser part of a pencil to push the bead so it centers in the hole.

The density of the outer shell varies with gourd varieties. I have noticed that cannonballs, apples, and copper canyon kettles have a harder, denser, and thinner shell surface than other gourd varieties. It was more difficult to push the beads into these gourds.

After teaching many classes using drilled holes and beads, I suggest the following tips:

· *Do not push the drill bit in the gourd more than once—multiple insertions will make the hole slightly larger.*

· *Keep the drill perpendicular to the gourd. Drilling at an angle makes pushing the bead in more difficult and results in a poor fit.*

· *Do not put a bead in and then push it all the way out. You have enlarged the hole and future beads will either be loose or fall through.*

· *If a hole is too large, wait until the gourd is finished and sealed; then glue the loose bead in place.*

Millimeters	Inches
1	3/64
2	5/64
3	1/8
4	5/32
5	13/64
6	15/64
7	9/32
8	5/16
9	23/64
10	25/64
11	7/16
12	15/32
13	33/64
14	35/64
15	19/32
16	5/8
17	43/64
18	45/64
19	3/4
20	25/32

DELICA F
SAM

Clear Solid Colors		Clear Rainbow Colors		Matte R
DP131		DP250		DP131FR
DP132		DP251		DP132FR
DP134		DP257		DP134FR
DP136		DP252		DP136FR
DP140		DP254		DP140FR
DP142		DP256		DP142FR
DP143		DP258		DP143FR
DP146		DP179		DP146FR
DP148		DP260		DP148FR
DP150		DP261		DP150FR
DP151		DP177		DP151FR
DP401				DP401FR
DP402		DP471		DP402FR

Cutting Out Designs

If you want a more complex design for your lamp than just holes, you can try carving or cutting out areas of the gourd. I use a MicroLux® Mini Jigsaw for cutting designs. The blade for a MicroLux fits into a ¹⁄₁₆" drilled starter hole. The saw can turn 360 degrees to create smooth clean curves. I also use sandpaper to finish any irregularly cut edges. The cut out area will expose the light. Be careful with your design since large cut outs will expose the light bulb.

See Through / Cover Up

If your design has large cut out areas that will show too much light, there are ways to hide the light bulb and/or soften the light. You can line the inside of the gourd with paper or fabric. There are wonderful choices of handmade papers and fabrics.

I collect old lampshades to use as an interior to some of my gourd shades. I look for "linen" type shades that I can either use as is, or color with the same ink or dye I used on the gourd. I cut the recycled shade into shapes to decoupage to the inside of my project.

Another way to hide the light bulb is to encase it in another gourd.

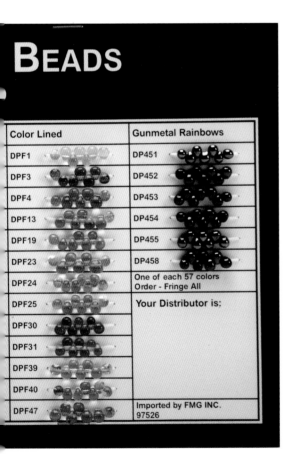

Color Lined		Gunmetal Rainbows	
DPF1		DP451	
DPF3		DP452	
DPF4		DP453	
DPF13		DP454	
DPF19		DP455	
DPF23		DP458	
DPF24		One of each 57 colors Order - Fringe All	
DPF25		Your Distributor is:	
DPF30			
DPF31			
DPF39			
DPF40			
DPF47		Imported by FMG INC. 97526	

BEADS

Removing Part of the Outer Shell

Depending on the thickness of the gourd you can remove the hard outer shell to create a soft (usually red) glow. The challenge is to remove the majority of the outer shell but not carve/cut all the way through. I recommend using a straight router bit with Dremel's Multipurpose Cutting Guide attachment. This two-part combination attachment came with all of my Dremel kits. I saw this attachment demonstrated at a carving technique class taught by Bonnie Gibson of Arizona Gourds. Dremel has straight router bits in the following sizes: ⅛", ³⁄₁₆", and ¼".

The rotary bit cuts flat bottoms and sharp side walls. The guide allows the user to adjust the depth of the cut and maintain some consistency. Because a gourd is naturally curved and has low spots / high plateaus the guide does not provide a consistent depth.

Gourds have a tendency to be thicker around the stem. If I am going to remove a section of the bottom of a gourd, I will keep that scrap to calculate a depth for my rotary guide. I had to practice to become proficient in keeping the flat guide on the curved portions of a gourd. It is my first step for removing part of the outer shell.

After carving out the initial area, I use a cylindrical toothed carbide burr. As I am left-handed, the nondirectional cutting helps me create a smoother surface on a gourd. I like the cylinder shape—it smoothes the sides as well as the bottom of the carved area. After the carbide, I use a cylindrical diamond bur and then sandpaper to create smooth carved out areas.

Drilling, cutting, and carving are some of the possibilities for creating textural designs on a gourd. I am sure there are other ways and different tools to create smooth carved areas on a gourd surface, but this combination works for me. Experiment to find your favorites.

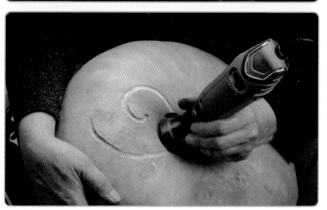

Basic Assembly

When I first considered writing a book on gourd lights, I started buying old lamps from estate sales, auctions, and thrift shops. I planned on just creating the shades, to avoid the electrical issues of wiring a lamp. Later, I realized that this book would be incomplete without a description of the process of building a lamp with its components. After taking an electrical wiring class at my local hardware store, I disassembled my collection of old lamps to learn all the components for making lamp fixtures. (See the Glossary.) Today I feel quite comfortable wiring a lamp, and you can too.

The first project is wiring a gourd for a lamp base. In fact, this project was so much fun, I started teaching classes at gourd festivals on these simple steps.

WIRING

CONNECT HOT AND NEUTRAL WIRES CORRECTLY!!!

If you wonder why you have to identify and connect the hot and neutral wires correctly in a lamp, read on. True, the lamp will usually work either way. But the issue is safety. Normally, power (voltage) comes through the tab on the socket base. The threaded socket is the neutral. So when the switch is off, all "hot" parts of the lamp are well protected. And when the switch is on, only the tab at the bottom of the socket is "hot." But if the wiring is reversed and the power goes to the threaded socket, the threaded socket is always hot, whether the switch is on or off. There's a much greater potential for getting a dangerous shock, especially when changing a bulb. The worst situation occasionally occurs in old fixtures when the cardboard insulation sleeve wears out and the outer metal shell of the socket touches the threaded socket. If the threaded socket is hot, every metallic part of the lamp becomes hot! Remember when repairing lamps, the neutral wire in the lamp cord is marked (usually with a rib or ribs) and it connects to the wide blade of the plug at one end and to the neutral screw (usually silver but may have some other identification) at the other end.

Source: http://www.familyhandyman.com/electrical/wiring/how-to-wire-a-light-socket/view-all#ixzz3ONv0NCtq

Basic Gourd Base

Materials Needed

Gourd
Threaded lamp pipe
Assorted locknuts and lock washers
SPT-2 plug and wire set
Socket
Harp
Finial
Check ring (optional)

Spindle or neck (optional)
Base (optional)
Lamp pipe flange (if using a base)
Hacksaw
Small Phillips-head screwdriver
Construction adhesive
Felt pad
Lead BBs (for weight)

1. Level the bottom of the gourd (I used an 8" disc sander).

2. Drill a ⅜" hole in the top (stem) and bottom (blossom).

3. If you are going to attach a base, make the bottom hole a little wider to cover the lamp pipe flange.

4. Screw the lamp pipe flange onto the base.

5. Thread cord through the base and up through the lamp pipe. (The pipe should already be cut to the height of the gourd plus approximately ⅓" for locknuts, harp, and socket.)

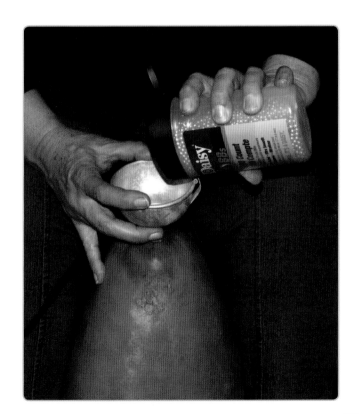

6. Add weight to the base (I use lead shot).

7. Thread a check ring through the cord. (This is an optional piece, but I like how it covers the top of the gourd.)

8. Thread a spindle through the cord. (This is an optional piece that adds height to the base.)

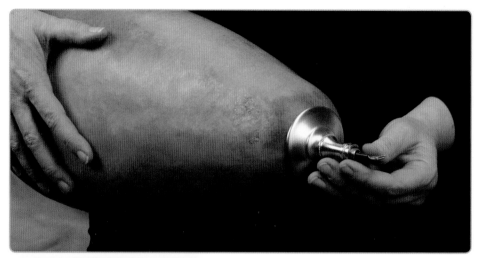

9. Thread the harp base through the cord.

10. Thread the socket base through the cord.

11. Tighten the screw on the socket base.

12. Identify the two wires in your cord. The neutral wire will have a ribbed plastic coating. It connects the wide blade of the plug and the neutral screw in the lamp socket. The neutral screw usually is silver. Wire this one first. Make sure there are no loose wires sticking out from the screw after you have tightened it.

Wrap the wire around the terminal screw in the direction you are going to use to tighten the screw.

After you have attached the neutral wire, repeat the process wiring the "hot" wire to the brass terminal screw.

PLEASE TAKE A MOMENT AND READ THE WIRING INSTRUCTIONS ABOUT THE IMPORTANCE OF WIRING CORRECTLY!

13. Before sliding the outer shell of the socket and locking it into the cap, test your lamp.

Twice I have built a lamp and discovered that it did not work (both times I had not tightened the terminal screws enough). I did discover that I had to destroy the outer socket shell to remove it.

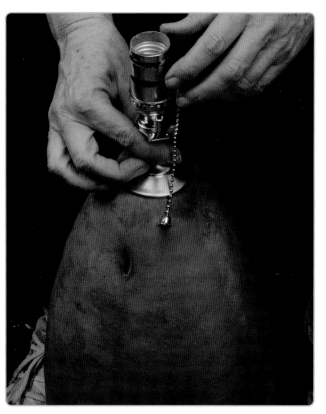

14. Glue the cord in the groove under the base.

15. Add self-adhesive felt to the base of the lamp.

Another way you could secure your cord is to tie a knot in the socket. This was difficult for me, so I opted to glue the cord in the base of the lamp.

16. Add the harp, lampshade, and finial and you have made your first gourd lamp.

Stacking Canteens

Materials Needed

Canteen gourds in assorted sizes
Howard Feed-N-Wax Wood Preserver
Threaded lamp pipe
Assorted locknuts and lock washers
SPT-2 plug and wire set
Socket
Harp
Finial

Check ring (optional)
Spindle or neck (optional)
Base (optional)
Lamp pipe flange (if using a base)
Hacksaw
Small Phillips-head screwdriver
Construction adhesive
Felt pad
Lead BBs

1. Choose your gourds.

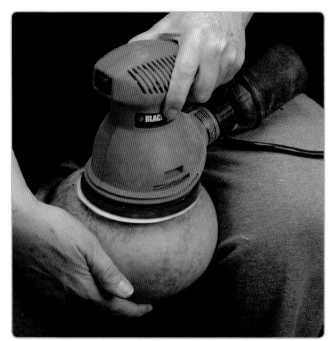

2. Smooth tops and bottoms for a tighter fit.

3. Seal with Howard Feed-N-Wax Wood Preserver.

4. Drill ⅜" holes through the tops and bottoms of all the gourds. (After drilling one canteen gourd you can position it on top of the next gourd to start your hole.)

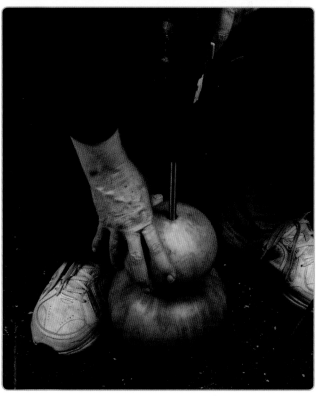

5. Screw a lamp pipe flange to a base and screw the lamp pipe into the flange.

6. Thread the cord up through the lamp pipe.

7. Thread the canteen gourds through the lamp pipe.

8. Identify and separate the two plastic coated wires and follow steps 7 through 16 in the Basic Gourd Base project.

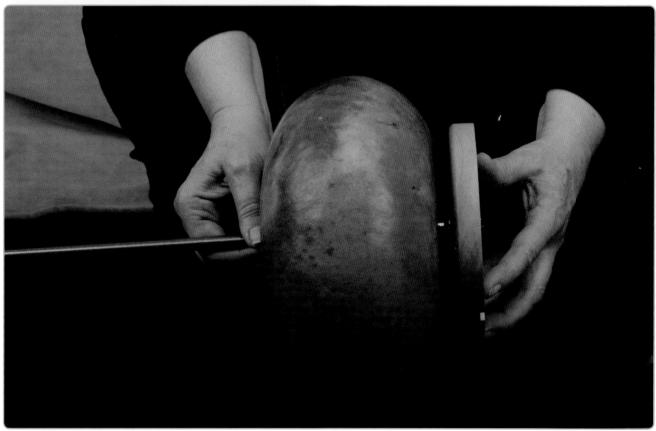

The gourd stack.

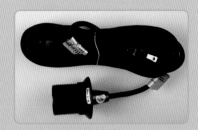

Using Pendant Kits

This book was inspired by the final project in *Cut-out Gourd Techniques*. I have taught a light workshop using the following 1,000 Holes project all over the country at gourd festivals, and even today other gourd instructors are teaching variations of that basic project.

I have included it in this book, but made it into a pendant light. The beauty of this project is that with either a simple design or a complex array of holes, the light will cast patterns all over nearby surfaces.

I was excited to find pendant kits at my local IKEA. They are easy to use and versatile. You do not have to wire them and they have the UL stamp of approval. The following projects will use the pendant for a hanging light fixture, a base for a table light, and then a wall sconce.

Pendant light kits are available from many sources. I buy mine from three sources:

> · *IKEA*
>
> · *Paper Lanterns Megastore (online)*
>
> · *World Market*

Each of the light kits requires a different size hole. Always make sure you measure your socket for a good fit.

1,000 Holes

Materials Needed

- Basketball gourd
- 1⅝" keyhole saw
- Paper Lanterns Megastore Pendant Kit
- Miriam Joy's Large Circle Craft Templates
- Drill and assorted drill bit sizes
- Howard Feed-N-Wax Wood Preserver

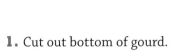

1. Cut out bottom of gourd.

2. Clean well.

3. Drill a 1⅜" opening for the light kit.

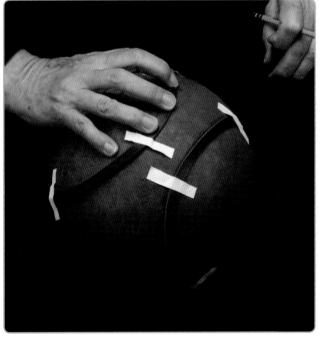

4. Draw your design. You can tape multiple rubber rings for visual placement. I draw the inside and outside of the ring.

5. Create a paper template for marking off hole placement around the circle.

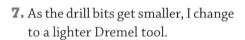

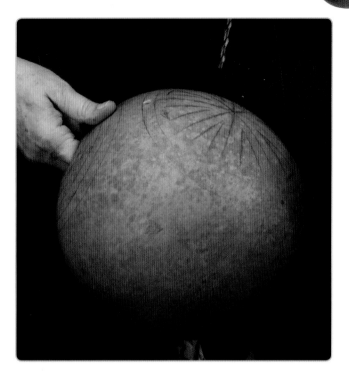

6. Start drilling with your largest drill bit. Try to stay perpendicular to the gourd.

7. As the drill bits get smaller, I change to a lighter Dremel tool.

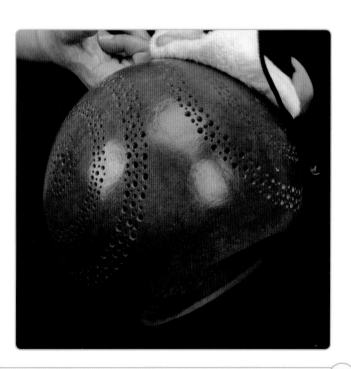

8. Wax and buff with Howard Feed-N-Wax Wood Preserver.

The finished project.

This is a versatile shape, originally created for a pendant light, but it fits perfectly on the lamp fixture I bought at Pottery Barn.

Cut-out Fern Swag

I love lights that reflect patterns. The fern stencil is a perfect choice to use for this pendant fixture. It is an easy pattern to cut out. The design is forgiving if you veer from the drawn pattern line. I have taught this project at gourd festivals and everyone raves about the reflected patterns on their hotel walls and ceilings!

Materials Needed

Gourd, bottom removed, cleaned inside and out
Stencil
Howard Feed-N-Wax Wood Preserver
Construction adhesive
Black Apoxie Sculpt®

25

Pendant light electrical kit.

1. Sand outside if the gourd has any rough surface area.

2. Draw freehand or use a stencil to outline the fern patterns.

3. Drill holes in all the fern pieces.

4. Insert saw and cut out each fern section.

5. Sand any cut edge that looks rough.

6. Drill a top hole sized to fit your pendant fixture.

7. Seal with Howard Feed-N-Wax Wood Preserver.

8. Feed cord through the top hole.

9. Because this gourd had a neck the shade screw would not work. I slid the cord up through the gourd and used construction adhesive to hold the cord and socket in place.

10. Pack the adhesive tightly and smooth off at the top.

11. To cover the neck hole I filled it with black Apoxie Sculpt.

The finished project.

Simple Table Light Bases

The last project resulted in a hanging pendant light. But what if you had that perfect place for a table lamp? Using the swag electrical light kit and a little ingenuity it is very easy to make a table lamp base. Since making my first base from some recycled wood, I have used driftwood, sliced logs, and a canteen gourd filled with weights. I confess that a friend of my family or one of my brothers cuts my circles.

Materials Needed

Scrap wood
Pendant light electrical kit

1. Cut a circle slightly larger than the gourd light.

2. Cut another circle 3" in diameter.

3. Drill a 1⅜" hole in the center of both circles (1⅜" works with the Paper Lantern Megastore Pendant kit).

4. Glue together.

The optional metal was added as an additional support to keep the swag in place.

5. Use a router to cut a groove for the cord. You could use some type of adhesive to permanently keep the cord in the grove, and then cover the bottom with felt.

6. Slide the unit through the holes and screw on the shade holder.

7. Make sure the hole in the bottom of the gourd will fit over the light bulb fixture.

After checking that everything fits, you can finish your base. I rounded the edges by sanding, painted the wood black for contrast, and decoupaged the edges. You could write a book on the many ways to finish the base. Just remember to seal it when finished.

Decorative Glow Wall Sconce

Materials Needed

Large canteen gourd
Pendant light electrical kit
Removable dot stickers (optional)
Drill and assorted sizes of hole saws and
    drill bits (I used 1¾", 1⅜", 1⅛", and ¾"
    hole saws and ½" and ⅜" drill bits)
Sandpaper

Adirondack Inks
Lacquer sealer
Marbled momi paper
Mod Podge®
Picture frame kit

1. Cut a large entrance circle on one side of the canteen gourd.

2. Clean well.

3. Arrange dots on the other side of the gourd. (This is an optional step. It's helpful for spacing the different sized holes evenly.)

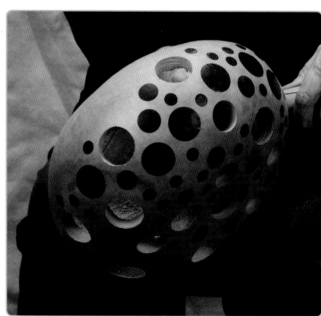

4. Drill all the holes, starting with the largest.

5. Drill a hole on the bottom for the pendant light kit.

6. Sand the edges of the holes.

7. Dye the gourd and edges of the holes using the Adirondack Inks.

8. Seal the gourd with the lacquer sealer.

The finished project.

9. Decoupage the interior of the gourd using Mod Podge.

10. Attach a wire for hanging.

11. Insert the pendant light.

Mike's Man Cave Wall Sconce

I created this for my brother's "man cave." I think it is going to fit perfectly with the rest of his décor.

Materials Needed

Large martin gourd
Pendant light electrical kit
Lauan plywood, ¼" thick
Stencil pattern
Removable vinyl
GourdMaster Rich Brown ink
Howard Feed-N-Wax Wood Preserver
Wood adhesive

1. Cut off one side of a martin gourd.

2. Drill a 1" hole in the remaining top portion of the gourd.

3. Cut out a backing for the sconce using luan or another lightweight piece of wood.

4. Cut a shelf to hold the pendant fixture.

5. Cut a hole in the center of the shelf that fits your pendant light.

6. Make sure everything fits snugly.

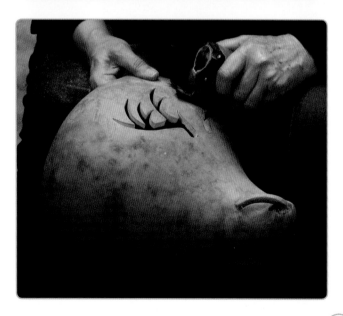

7. Use removable vinyl to place your stenciled design on the light and trace.

8. Cut out your design.

9. Color your gourd. I used GourdMaster's Rich Brown ink.

10. Seal the gourd with Howard Feed-N-Wax Wood Preserver.

11. Thread the plug portion of the pendant light unit through the hole in the gourd.

12. Slide the unit through the shelf hole and screw on the shade holder.

13. Glue the back onto the gourd. I used a combination of Bob Smith Industries® (BSI) quick super glue and construction adhesive. I taped it to hold it while drying.

The finished project.

Lamp Shades

After making my first lamp base I went looking for a commercial lamp shade and discovered I had a dilemma similar to Goldilocks: some were "too big," others "too small," but I was lucky to find one that was "ahh just right." I never found a definite formula for lamp base to shade, but the basic rule of thumb when measuring the entire height of the lamp is 60% base and 40% shade. The other consideration is the width, the shade being twice as wide as the base. But the best part of researching on the Internet is how many sites you can find that will say "break the guidelines, go with your heart."

When making a gourd base and a shade it takes awhile to find that perfect combination. On the image shown here the shade is too small for the gourd lamp base. I'm still looking for the bottom base that will complement my shade.

Basic Lamp Shade

Materials needed

    Large kettle gourd
    Spider

I wanted to design a lamp shade like the majority of commercial shades you can buy today. With both the top and bottom open, the shade allows air to flow freely. The shades are usually wired inside for easy attachment to the top of a harp and secured with a finial.

To attach the open gourd shade we are going to use a lamp part called a spider. It is a very interesting piece that replaces a lamp harp. The gourd shade will rest on the spider's outstretched arms. You could attach a metal or wooden ball to the spider's wires. You could attach mini gourds to the spider. Spiders come in different sizes. You can even buy the center ring and add your own wires.

Here are the simple steps to create your shade. It will be up to you to decide how to enhance and embellish the shade.

1. Cut out the top and bottom of the gourd.

2. Clean and sand the outside and inside for a smooth finish.

3. Sand the top and bottom edges for a smooth and level look. I started with a orbital sander and finished with a sanding board.

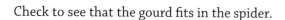

Check to see that the gourd fits in the spider.

One of the problems I have is figuring out where to cut the lamp pipe to have that optimum distance between lamp base and shade. For this project I decided to create an adjustable spider.

I attached a series of knurl (decorative) locknuts on the lamp pipe. This allowed me to adjust the spider height by spinning the locknuts up or down. You only need locknuts to hold the spider securely, but I added the others for a decorative element.

Cut-out Oak Leaves Lamp Shade

I love making cut-out leaf designs. I am comfortable with the leaf overlays, so I thought I would create a lampshade using the same techniques I use in creating the oak leaf bowls. I am very happy with the results and my new lamp fits perfectly in my eclectic home.

Materials Needed

Large bushel basket gourd
Paper leaf patterns
Memories® Inks
Sponge daubers
Brown dye
Deft® Satin Lacquer spray
Mod Podge®
Marbled momi paper

There is always the basic prep work for any gourd project.

1. Clean and sand the outside of the gourd.

2. Cut an opening and clean inside of the gourd, making it as smooth as possible.

3. Coat the inside of the gourd with a glue/paint mixture. I do this step to strengthen the gourd. You could also use a wood stabilizer.

4. Draw an all-over design.

5. Drill holes in open spaces. Insert your blade and cut out the spaces around the leaves. I did not cut the bottom edge.

6. Carve veins using a rotary tool and a small round bur.

7. Remove gourd dust with a hair dryer or leaf blower.

8. Color the leaves. I used Memories Inks (yellow, orange, brown, pinetree green, and port red) and Tsukineko Sponge Daubers.

9. Paint the cut out edges with brown dye. I used dark brown Fiebing's Oil Dye.

10. Finish cutting the edge of the lampshade. Dye and paint any unfinished areas.

11. Spray with a satin sealer.

After completing the shade, I decided that the cut-outs showed too much of the light and socket fixtures. I decided to decoupage the inside of the shade.

12. Decoupage inside the gourd lamp shade for a softer glow.

I trimmed the decoupage area back leaving a few cut-outs along the bottom edge of the shade. I love the shadow that it makes. This is one of my favorites.

Gallery of Contributing Artists

I am sometimes asked, "What do you see as the future for this technique (gourd lights)?"

I always answer the same way: "You know that expression 'the future is now!'? When I look at today's work, I am overwhelmed by the gourd lights that are being created. I'm not even sure I can narrow down the list of the artisans who have inspired me most."

The following are artisans from around the world who are creating functional lights that are also inspiring works of art.

Mehmet Ali Aydin

Mehmet Ali, reachable via the Su Kabağı Müzesi gourd museum in Alanya, Turkey, was a major inspiration for me in my gourd lamp work. I remember placing my first order for 400,000 beads with Mehmet Ali and wondering, "What am I doing?" Here are four of my favorites among his beaded light gourds.

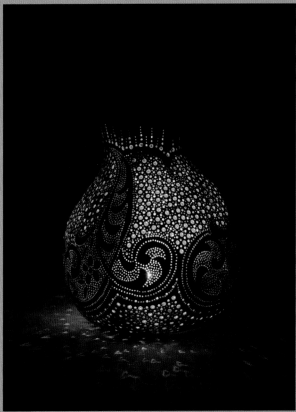

Reagan Bitler

Reagan is an up and coming gourd artist in Hanover, York County, Pennsylvania. Reagan's pieces often feature the use of dark pyrography lines, cut outs, and the incorporation of unique embellishment materials. His finished pieces can be found in consignment shops in northern Pennsylvania and at several art and craft shows throughout the year.

Reagan has taught gourd classes at Maryland Gourd Days and the Pennsylvania Gourd Gathering. He has served as the president of the Pennsylvania Gourd Society and actively participates with the Harford Community College gourd group and the Mason-Dixon gourd patch. In his non-gourding life, Reagan works full time as an eighth grade social studies teacher for the Hanover Public School District.

Adriana Jacob

After more than thirty years as an artistic painter, five years ago Adriana discovered how gourds could develop her art and...she was fascinated.

"The versatility and nobility of the gourd inspires me to capture Mexican colors, which are my passion. Vibrant, cheerful, passionate, life-full colors—I mix them to create designs based on the culture, crafts, and customs of my Mexico. Painting, cutting, carving in gourds has focused my imagination to create unique, different pieces to brighten the view and the space where they are placed."

"Xitlalli-pan, The Gourd as Art" is an artisan workshop in the community of Jolalpan, Puebla, Mexico, where Adriana is initiating a cooperative with local people and producers who cultivate gourds in that area. "We are starting production of modern and innovative Mexican crafts made of this ancient fruit." www.facebook.com/adriana.jacob.393

Przemek Krawczyński

Przemek, the founder and sole producer of the Calabarte brand of gourd lamps, lives and works in Łódź, Poland. He started designing and creating gourd lamps in 2009 when he accidently came across gourds. After a trip to Senegal, the African round calabashes have become a basic and favorite material for his lamps.

Meanwhile, Przemek had been studying engineering and working at an architectural studio, but in 2010 he decided to quit both, and to devote himself solely to the creation of gourd lamps.

His science background results in complicated patterns inspired by geometry, fractals, nature, or the works of M. C. Escher and Ernst Haeckel. The creation of one lamp takes around three months of continuous mental and manual work. www.calabarte.com

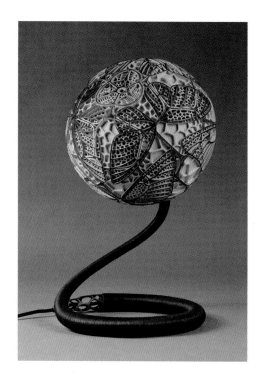

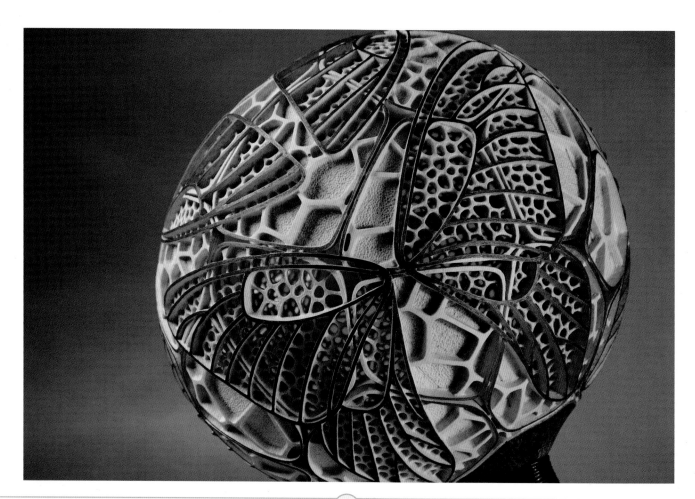

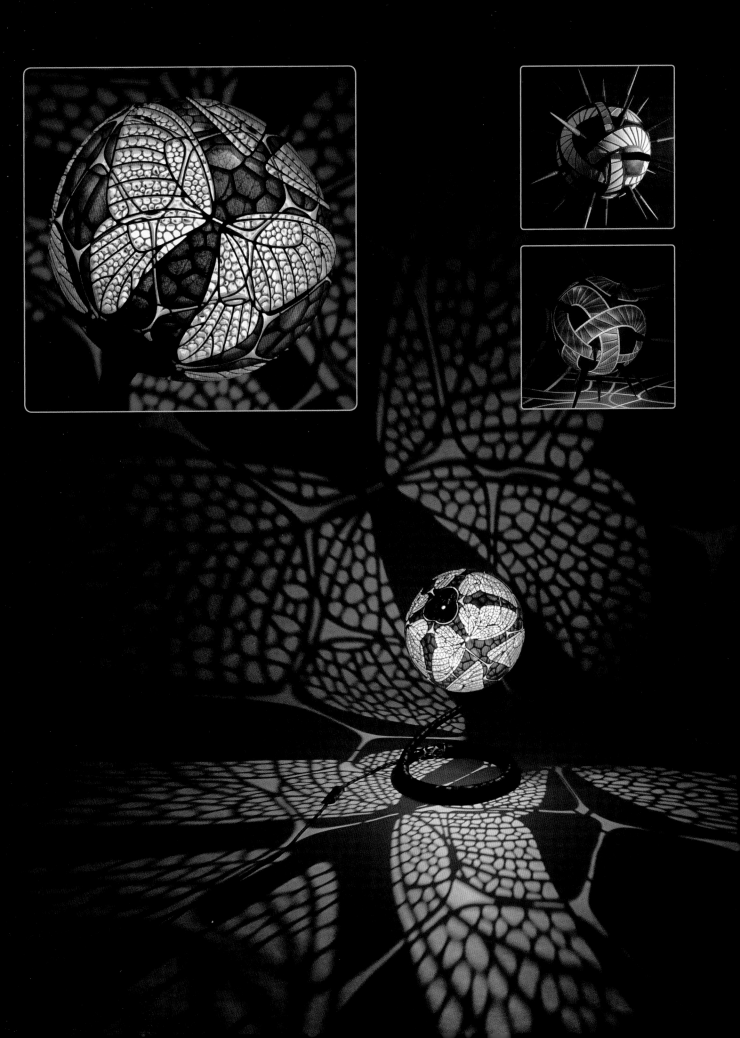

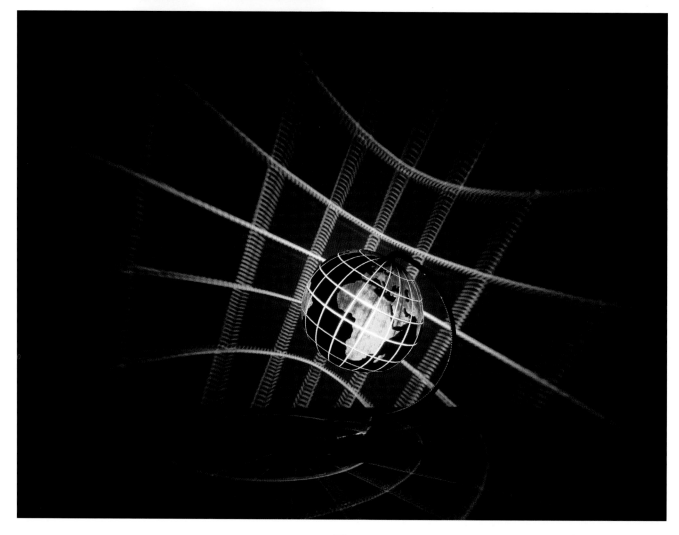

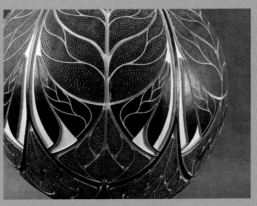
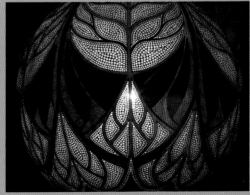

59

Jane Mawson

Jane is a third generation artist living in Chestnut Hill, Pennsylvania. Jane takes inspiration from the Bauhaus tradition of unifying art and craft, design and function, in her work. Her process is organic and free-form. Jane has shown her work in several galleries in the Philadelphia area.

Dan McNamara

Dan's creations include musical instruments made from gourds (guitars, harps, lyres, ukeleles, flutes, drums, and rain sticks). Dan is always looking for something different to make from a gourd.

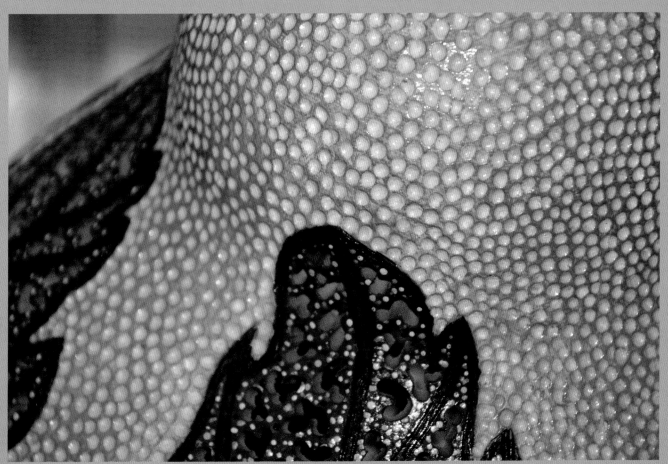

Graham Ottoson

Graham Ottoson, self-proclaimed Queen of Gourdlandia, was introduced to gourdcrafting by a fellow midwife several years ago. Having dabbled in everything from stained glass to paper-mache, watercolor, gingerbread (serious gingerbread), and more, Graham was happy to find one medium that requires so many different skills.

She enjoys the simple tasks of cleaning and scraping, staining and waxing, as much as designing and carving. She loves her teeny jigsaw (as big as a bar of soap!), and her collection of rasps and drill bits.

Graham and her husband Otto enjoy summer evenings of hand-pollinating the beautiful white blossoms and nurturing the tiny pepos gourds on the vine. The vertical design on many of her lamps stems from observation of how gourds grow.

Graham's business, Gourdlandia, is a highlight on the Greater Ithaca Art Trail.

JoAnne Phelps

A native Marylander, JoAnne is a self-taught artist. She has a love for many fine arts, and her woodworking includes small furniture, scroll work, turning, and carving, which she recently has been doing on watermelons as well as on gourds. She finds gourds to be a fabulous medium in that they allow her to combine many techniques, such as wood-burning, carving, painting, and various 3-D applications.

Ron Poole

Carving is a family tradition in the Poole family, and as a child Ron would watch his grandfather carve kachina dolls using hand tools; his father, a trained commercial artist, carved walking sticks. Ron's gourd lamps are inspired by patterns found in nature, from sea life to the cosmos to the neural structures of the brain. His work has been shown in galleries in Michigan, Indiana, and Utah.

"TAMAMIZU"
by
R. Poole

Kyle Rowlands

Kyle was introduced to gourd art through a class taught by the author. She lives in Havre de Grace, Maryland, with her husband Rob who indulges her love of gourding through classes, festivals far and wide, and an ever-expanding collection of gourds that seem to multiply in the night.

Robin Carter Weathersby

Robin was born in the mountains of western North Carolina. She moved to several states while serving in the military, but the Appalachian and Blue Ridge Mountains are her home and inspiration.

Robin's fascination with gourds began when she saw a photo of a gourd bowl. She found a local gourd grower, and has since become a gourd light artist.

"Adding light to a work adds a new dimension to the art; it is transformed and so is the room! It's like getting multiple pieces of art in one. During the day you can see the stains, the beautiful colors of the gourd, the intricacy of the design, but at night all you see is the light and its effect on the room. It is breathtaking."

Robin has won Best in Show at the 2014 Festival in the Park in Charlotte, North Carolina. She is a proud sponsor of local artists and helps to promote youth art in her community. You can find her at www.2sistersliving art.com.

GALLERY OF CONTRIBUTING ARTISTS

Glossary

Gourd artisans are creating incredible lamps and light fixtures, but sometimes struggle with naming and finding the correct electrical components to finish their project. Many homeowners have vintage lamps they would like to rewire, as well. The next two sections will help anyone with lamp construction.

Base: The bottom portion of a lamp. A base adds weight for stability, can be a decorative finishing touch, and can provide a side hole for the cord. You can buy bases made of a variety of materials or you can make one out of found objects (rocks, limbs, antlers, etc.). I once used a canteen gourd filled with stones and resin as a base.

Cap, Check Ring: A decorative piece used to cover and reduce the openings at the ends of pipes so that any threaded stem can be held firmly in place. Caps will also cover up a larger hole in the base portion of the lamp. You can find check rings made from a variety of metals and wood. Commercial check rings are threaded to fit standard IP pipes. You can also use another gourd as a check ring as a decorative element.

Chain: Used for swag lights to help support weight as well as provide a decorative element.

Cord: A standard lamp cord has two plastic coated wires called 18/2 (2 wires, 18 size). Every cord has a neutral wire. The neutral wire usually has a rib or series of ribs. The neutral wire connects the wide blade of the plug and the neutral screw in the lamp socket. Once you have identified the neutral wire, the other wire is the "hot" wire. For convenience lamp cords are sold with plugs molded to the cord.

Coupling: Used to combine two pieces of lamp pipe. Couplings are short fittings that have two female ends. You can also find couplings that connect two different sized lamp pipes.

Finial: A decorative piece that usually screws to the top of a harp. A finial provides stability for the shade. You can find finials that fit a standard 1/8 IP lamp pipe.

Harp: The part that holds the shade. Harps are made in heights from 7 to 12" in steps of ½", and (in steps of whole inches) to 15". There is an extended threaded piece above the arch of the harp for attaching a decorative finial. The height of a harp is measured from the base (under the socket) to the finial base. You can find your harp measurement labeled under the finial base at the top of the harp.

If you already have a harp but want to raise your shade, consider using a riser.

Lamp Pipe Flange: A connector that attaches a lamp pipe to a lamp base with two screws. After the flange is attached to the lamp base, the lamp pipe can be screwed into the threaded part of the flange.

Loader, Weight: An attachment to the base of a lamp to add weight. Loaders come in different sizes and weights. They have a center hole to slip down a pipe and a slot for the lamp cord to lay flat.

Locknut and Lock washer: Used to secure different components of the lamp, especially the lamp pipe. These are specialty items; ordinary nuts and washers won't work. You can use hexagonal locknuts and palnuts in situations where they won't be visible. There are decorative locknuts for use when they will be visible. An example would be a locknut between the base and the socket of a lamp.

Neck, Spindle: Decorative pieces to add height between the body of a lamp and the socket. Necks are usually smaller in height, less than 2"; spindles are taller, up to 4½". You can add any combination to reach a particular height.

Nipple: Short piece of threaded pipe used when the lamp pipe is too short. You can add a nipple to the main pipe by using a coupling.

Non-abrasive Self-adhesive Felt: Provides a protective, non-scratch barrier between surfaces. It is very easy to use. It can be cut to size and shape. After cutting, peel off the paper backing and press into place.

Plug and Wire Set: A cord set with in-line switch and molded-on polarized plug. Underwriters Laboratories (UL) listings recommend SPT-2 lamp cord sets for table and floor lamps as they have heavier outside plastic covering than traditional SPT-1 cords. The heavier outside covering on SPT-2 lamp cord sets may make it harder to slip 1/8 IP lamp pipe when threading lamps. I use plug and wire sets because they provide a seamless connection at the plug end.

As with lamp sockets, UL issues standards for lamp cord manufacturers that specify wire gauge (size) and insulation thickness/durability. These specifications are usually stamped or appear in small print on lamp cords, plugs, and sockets.

The SPT refers to the insulation around the copper wires, which protects a person from being shocked and protects the cord from fraying. These three SPT ratings and recommendations from B&P Lamp Supplies (www.bplampsupply.com) are useful as a guide.

SPT-1: This wire is UL Listed for use in hanging fixtures and sconces. Easily slips 1/8 IP (⅜" dia.) pipe.
SPT-1 1/2: This wire is UL Listed for use in fixtures hanging by a chain. Easily slips 1/8 IP (⅜" dia.) pipe.
SPT-2: This wire is UL Listed for use in portable table and floor lamps. Difficult to slip 1/8 IP (⅜" dia.) pipe.

Shade Riser: Used to "raise" the shade or the finial. To raise the shade, screw the riser onto the stud of the harp before you add the shade. To raise the finial, add the riser after placing the shade on the stud of the harp.

Socket: The "bulb holder" has not changed much in the last hundred years. Construction and materials used to create lamp sockets are regulated by Underwriters Laboratories (UL) and are referred to as "lampholders." There are many sockets on the market made for different uses but the construction is the same. Sockets can be made out of metal, porcelain, or plastic. There are sockets that have switches or no switch at all (keyless, push through, pull chain, key turn).

The socket's most important feature is that it provides the electrical connection to the bulb. On most sockets the power (voltage) comes through the tab at the base of the socket. If wired correctly only the tab is "hot."

LAMP SOCKET TERMINOLOGY

Cap: The exterior base of the socket. The cap locks into the shell and is threaded to fit lamp pipes.

Outer Shell: The exterior top of the lamp socket. The outer shell locks into the base.

Cardboard Shell: An insulation layer between the outer shell and inner shell.

Inner Shell: Thread socket that has the two terminal screws (one brass, one nickel), and the metal tab that connects to the light bulb.

 Spider (tripod, shade holder): A metal ring that slips over a lamp pipe to fit under the lamp socket. The ring has three arms that extend out to support a shade. Spiders were originally designed to hold a glass shade, but can easily be converted to hold a gourd. Spiders or tripods have three arms. A shade holder has a continuous ring.

 **Threaded lamp pipe:** The core of most lamps. The lamp pipe provides a channel for wiring as well as a stable base to hold the socket. Lamp pipes come in different sizes but the standard sizes are 1/8 IP (table lamps) and 1/4 IP (floor lamps). 1/8 and 1/4 do not refer to the diameter of the pipe. IP stands for "iron pipe" and the sizes reflect the nineteenth-century Briggs Standard of Wrought-Iron Pipe Dimensions. A 1/8 IP pipe has a 0.405" outer diameter, fits in a 7/16" hole, and is threaded 27 threads to the inch. You can buy precut lamp pipe that is only threaded at each end. Since I never know the length I need, I buy 36" continuous threaded pipe. All thread lamp pipe is easily cut with a hacksaw.

Tubing: A decorative covering for the lamp pipe. You need ½" tubing to slip over a 1/8 IP pipe.

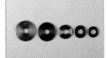 **Vase Caps:** Decorative item for the top of a lamp base. The center hole slips 1/8 IP standard lamp pipe. You can find vase caps in a wide variety of metals, pottery, and wood.

Resources

Sources for Lamp Parts

Antique Lamp Supply
McMinnville, TN
931-473-1906
www.antiquelampsupply.com

lampdoctor.blogspot.com

My Lamp Parts
Chicago, IL
773-539-7910
www.mylampparts.com

National Artcraft Co.
Aurora, OH
330-562-3500
www.nationalartcraft.com

Paxton Hardware
Upper Falls, MD
1-800-241-9741
www.paxtonhardware.com

Professional Hardware and Supply Co.
Casa Grande, AZ
1-800-248-1919
www.profhdwr.com

Texas Lamp Parts
Forney, TX
972-564-5267
www.txlampparts.net

Raw Gourd Suppliers

Beiler's Gourds
Lancaster, PA
717-687-8797

Ghost Creek Gourds
Laurens, SC
864-682-5251
www.ghostcreekgourds.com
rmartin@backroads.net

Pumpkin Hollow
Piggott, AR
870-598-3568
www.pumpkinhollow.com
ellen@pumpkinhollow.com

Smucker's Gourd Farm
Kinzers, PA
717-354-6118

Welburn Gourd Farm
Fallbrook, CA
877-420-2613
www.welburngourdfarm.com

Wuertz Gourd Farm
Casa Grande, AZ
520-723-4432
www.wuertzfarm.com
wuertzfarm@wuertzfarm.com

Gourding Supplies

Arizona Gourds
Tucson, AZ
www.arizonagourds.com

Blue Whale Arts
Epping, NH
603-679-1961
www.bluewhalearts.com

The Caning Shop
Berkeley, CA
1-800-544-3373
www.caning.com

Craft Supplies
Provo, UT
1-800-551-8876
www.woodturnerscatalog.com

Gourd Market
Baldwin, MD
www.shop.gourdmarket.com/main.sc

Bibliography

Bryan Reid, Susan, ed. *Light and Electricity*. Chicago: St. Remy Press, 1997.

Burton, Ken. *Crafting Wooden Lamps*. Blue Ash, OH: Popular Woodworking Books, 2011.

Coggins, Frank W. *All About Lamps: Construction, Repair and Restoration*. Blue Ridge Summit, PA: Tab Books, 1986.

Hiebert, Helen. *Paper Illuminated*. North Adams, MA: Storey Publishing, 2001.

Martens, Rachel. *The How-To Book of Repairing, Rewiring and Restoring Lamps and Lighting Fixtures*. Garden City, NY: Doubleday & Company, Inc., 1979.

Myerson, Jeremy, and Sylvia Katz. *Lamps and Lighting*. New York: Van Nostrand Reinhold, 1990.

Susan (Suzi) Nonn, artisan and author, loves gourds—their shapes, their mold patterns, even their defects. She has worked with gourds for more than twenty years and, through her classes and coaching, encourages others to try gourd crafting. Nonn teaches gourd workshops at Harford Community College (Bel Air, Maryland) and at gourd festivals across the United States. She is the coordinator for the Gourd Gathering at Cherokee (Cherokee, North Carolina). Nonn is also the author of *Cut-out Gourd Techniques,* a book written to help gourd artists to improve their skills with the mini-saw. When not teaching, she can be found in her studio/garage enhancing gourds.